Contents

Cocoon Entwined

1

Yuriko Hara

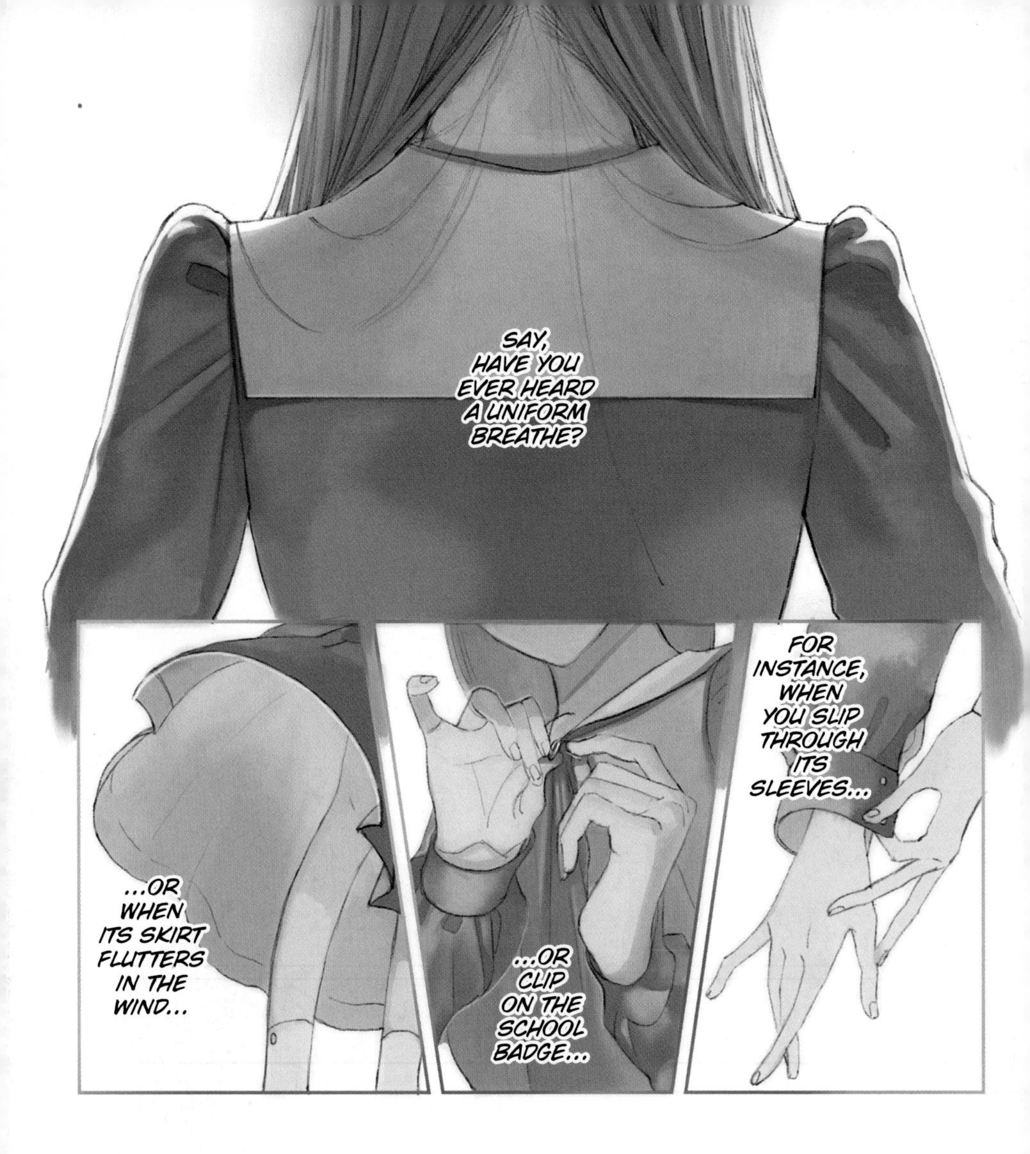
SAY, HAVE YOU EVER HEARD A UNIFORM BREATHE?
FOR INSTANCE, WHEN YOU SLIP THROUGH ITS SLEEVES...
...OR CLIP ON THE SCHOOL BADGE...
...OR WHEN ITS SKIRT FLUTTERS IN THE WIND...
YOU THINK I'M BEING SILLY, DON'T YOU?
BUT YOU KNOW WHAT? AT THIS HIGH SCHOOL, IT ACTUALLY HAPPENS.

BECAUSE OUR UNIFORMS ARE......
CHAPTER 1

TWO HOURS FROM THE CITY BY TRAIN, YOU'LL SEE TWO BIG WHITE OAK TREES THAT MAKE IT APPEAR AS IF THE FOREST HAS TWO HATS ON.

SIGN: HOSHIMIYA ACADEMY

A SMALL PATH UNFOLDS UNDER THE WHITE OAKS' WATCH...
...LEADING INTO A FOREST DENSE ENOUGH TO HIDE A SECRET PARADISE.
THEREIN LIES OUR HOSHIMIYA GIRLS' ACADEMY.

3-A
GOOD-BYE.
BYE.
3-B
WE'VE REACHED THE END OF THE SCHOOL DAY, BUT THIS IS IMPORTANT, SO PLEASE PAY ATTENTION UNTIL THE VERY END.

ONCE WINTER BREAK DRAWS TO A CLOSE, THE UNIFORM-MAKING WILL BEGIN.
I SUSPECT MORE THAN A FEW OF YOU ENROLLED IN OUR SCHOOL EXPRESSLY FOR THIS UNIFORM.

THE HIGH SCHOOL DIVISION'S UNIFORMS HAVE A LONG HISTORY.
THE YOUNG WOMEN WHO ATTENDED THIS SCHOOL YEARS PRIOR—YOUR PREDECESSORS—ALL SOUGHT TO PRESERVE THE TRADITION OF MAKING UNIFORMS TO PASS DOWN TO THE INCOMING FIRST-YEARS.
THE GIRLS OF THE MIDDLE SCHOOL DIVISION ARE EAGERLY AWAITING YOUR UNIFORMS.
FOR DECEMBER, IT'S A WARM AFTERNOON.
カサ
KASA (CRINKLE)
SAMPLE PATTERN
ON DAYS LIKE TODAY...
DO YOUR BEST TO CREATE EXCELLENT UNIFORMS THAT LIVE UP TO THE WHITE OAK TREES THAT HAVE WATCHED OVER YOU GIRLS.
...MY UNIFORM FEELS ELATED.

TODAY'S CLASS HELPER IS...
OH DEAR. IT'S HOSHIMIYA-SAN?

HMM... THEN...
きょろ
KYORO
きょろ
KYORO (GLANCE)
ソソ
SOSO (SNEAK)

YOKO-ZAWA-SAN.

YES, MA'AM ......

THAT OLD BAT!

WHY IS IT ALWAYS ME?
THERE ARE PLENTY OF OTHER GIRLS WITH NOTHING BETTER TO DO!

PI (SNAG)
WHOA, WHOA!
YOUR HAIR ALMOST GOT CAUGHT.
SAEKI-SAN!
THAT WON'T DO, YOKOZAWA-SAN.
AFTER ALL, YOUR HAIR IS VERY BEAUTIFUL.
CHU (KISS)

キャー!!
キャ
SQUEEEEE!!
I'LL HELP YOU CARRY THAT.
...... THANKS.
GOING TO THE DRESSMAKING BUILDING?
YEAH.

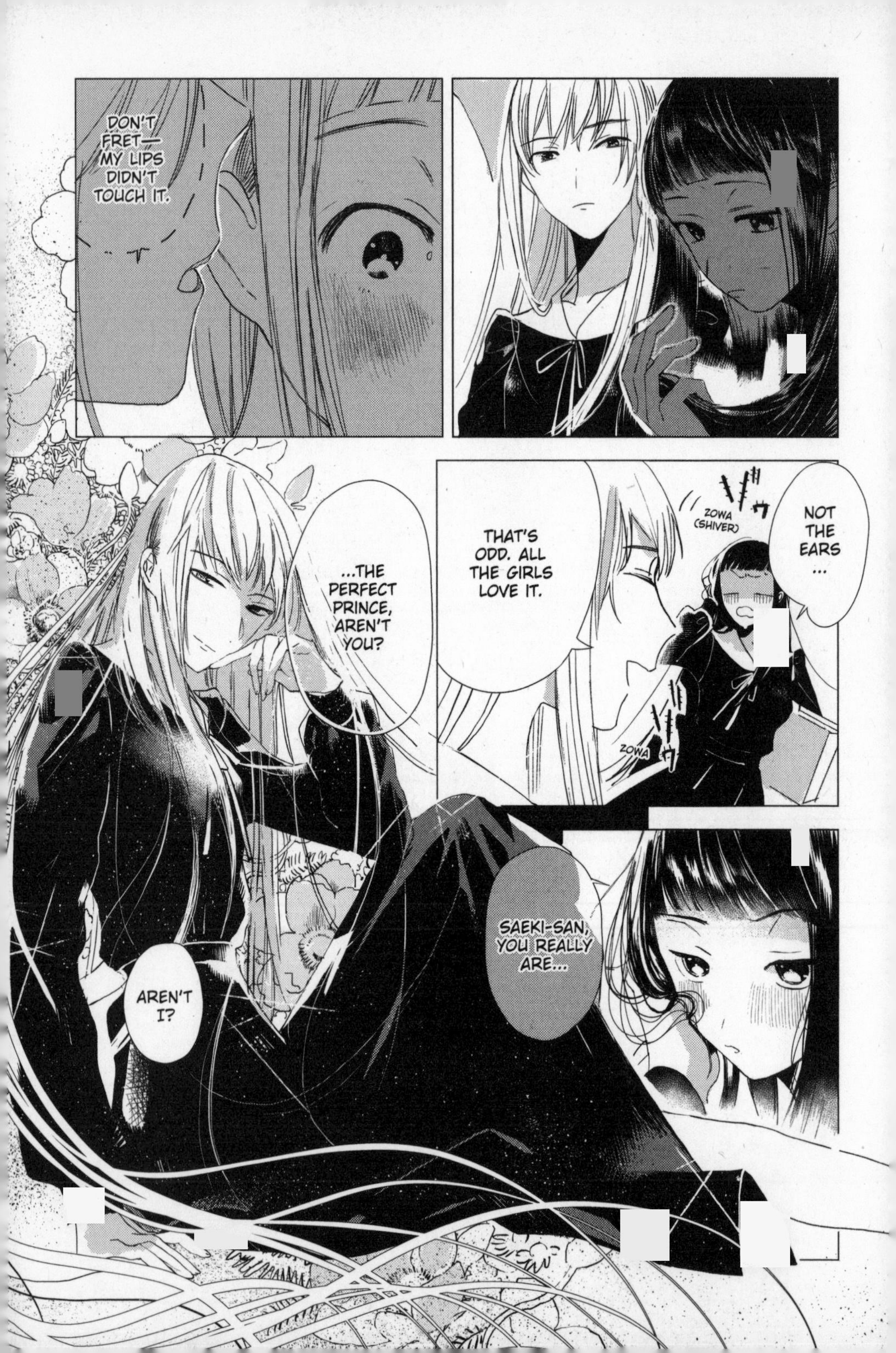
DON'T FRET—MY LIPS DIDN'T TOUCH IT.
NOT THE EARS...
ZOWA (SHIVER)
THAT'S ODD. ALL THE GIRLS LOVE IT.
ZOWA
SAEKI-SAN, YOU REALLY ARE...
...THE PERFECT PRINCE, AREN'T YOU?
AREN'T I?

SO YOU'LL HAVE SHORT HAIR IN THE THIRD TERM TOO?
YOU'LL BE EVEN MORE PRINCE-LIKE THEN.
HA HA!
MY THOUGHTS EXACTLY.
OH YEAH?
OH REALLY...?
YOU MIGHT AS WELL CALL ME A STUD.

BY THE WAY, YOU AREN'T ON CLASS DUTY TODAY, ARE YOU?
HOSHIMIYA-SAN IS.
AH... SHE DIDN'T SHOW UP TO CLASS?
IT SEEMS LIKE SOMEONE SAW HER IN THE LIBRARY.
"SEEMS"?
WELL, LATELY, SHE'S SHUT HERSELF UP IN THE DORM AND WON'T COME OUT.
HER WINDOW'S OPEN, SO SHE'S PROBABLY ALIVE.

SHE MIGHT BE THE HEAD-MISTRESS'S GRANDDAUGHTER AND ALL, BUT THE TEACHERS ARE EVEN STAYING OFF HER CASE.
THE LADY OF THE COCOON.

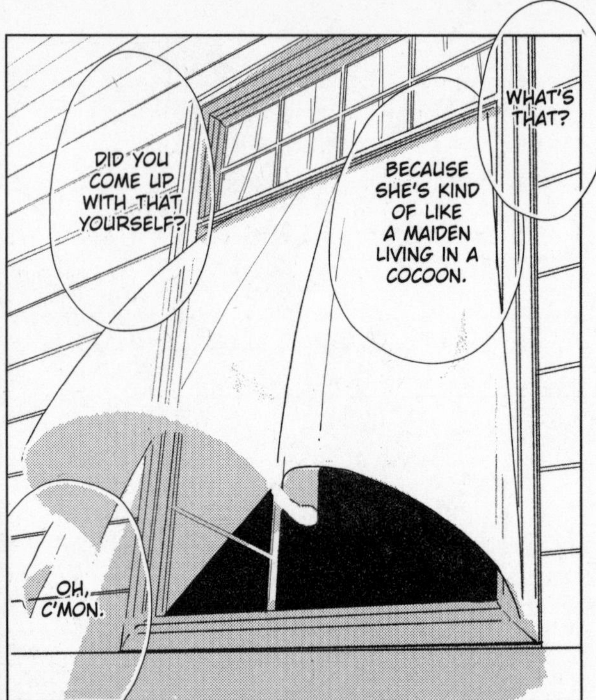
WHAT'S THAT?
BECAUSE SHE'S KIND OF LIKE A MAIDEN LIVING IN A COCOON.
DID YOU COME UP WITH THAT YOURSELF?
OH, C'MON.

I ONLY HEARD IT TOO.

被服棟

SIGN: DRESSMAKING BUILDING

FUAAA (YAWN)
IF THEY SAW YOU LIKE THAT, ALMOST ANY GIRL WOULD SNAP OUT OF EVEN THE DEEPEST LOVE.
TOKU (MELT)
D'YOU THINK?
DOING THE DAZZLING, DASHING PRINCE ACT ALL THE TIME IS EXHAUSTING.
AND BESIDES...

...I DON'T SHOW THIS SIDE OF ME TO ANY OTHER GIRLS...
...DO I, YOUKO?
WHY IS HANA-SAN'S FACE THE ONLY GOOD THING...
...ABOUT HER?
I CAN HEAR YOUUU.

WHAT?

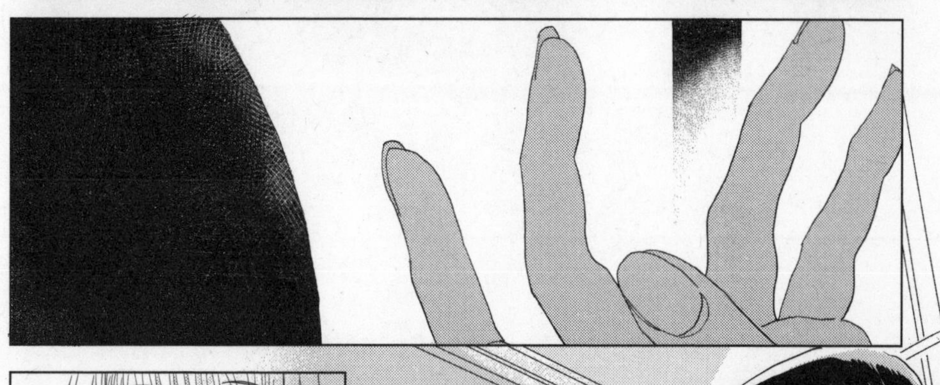

I JUST FELT THIS UNIFORM BREATHE.

BREATHE?

OH YEAH, I THINK I'VE HEARD OF THAT.
I ALWAYS WROTE IT OFF AS AN URBAN LEGEND OR SOMETHING.

MY UNIFORM ESPECIALLY... IS LINKED TO MY HEART.
WHETHER IT'S HAPPY...
...OR TIRED...
...I CAN SENSE ITS EMOTIONS.
YOU'RE CREEPED OUT, RIGHT?
HOW ABOUT IT? CAN YOU TELL HOW IT FEELS?
EVEN IF YOU ASK...
...I CAN'T TELL WITH SOMEONE ELSE'S.
C'MON, PLEASE?

I'LL TRY, BUT DON'T EXPECT ANY-THING.
THANKS.
HAAH...

BUT...
...THIS UNIFORM REALLY IS GORGEOUS.

YOU KNOW...

...I ENROLLED AT THIS SCHOOL BECAUSE I WANTED TO MAKE THIS UNIFORM.

I WONDER WHAT KIND OF GIRL THE ONE I MAKE WILL GO TO.

MM-HM.

AS LONG AS SHE'LL CHERISH IT, THAT'S ENOUGH FOR ME, BUT...AREN'T YOU AWFULLY CURIOUS?

HEY, WHAT KIND OF GIRL DO YOU...?
UH-HUH.
DID YOU THINK I HADN'T NOTICED...
...THAT WHEN YOU LOOK AWAY FROM ME...

...YOU'RE GAZING AT THAT WINDOW, WITH THE FACE OF A PRINCE?

"I'M SOOO TIRED"— THAT'S WHAT IT'S SAYING.
JUST QUIT BEING A PRINCE.
AH.
I'VE DONE IT NOW ......
BUT I WON'T APOLOGIZE.
POSU (FWUMP)
ぽす。

HUH?
THIS UNI-FORM ...

...HAS TWO BREATHS......?

LONG AGO, THERE WAS A BIG WAR.
THE WAR TOOK MANY THINGS.
LAUGHTER WITH OTHERS, MOURNING, LOVED ONES...
...AND EVEN CLOTHING ......

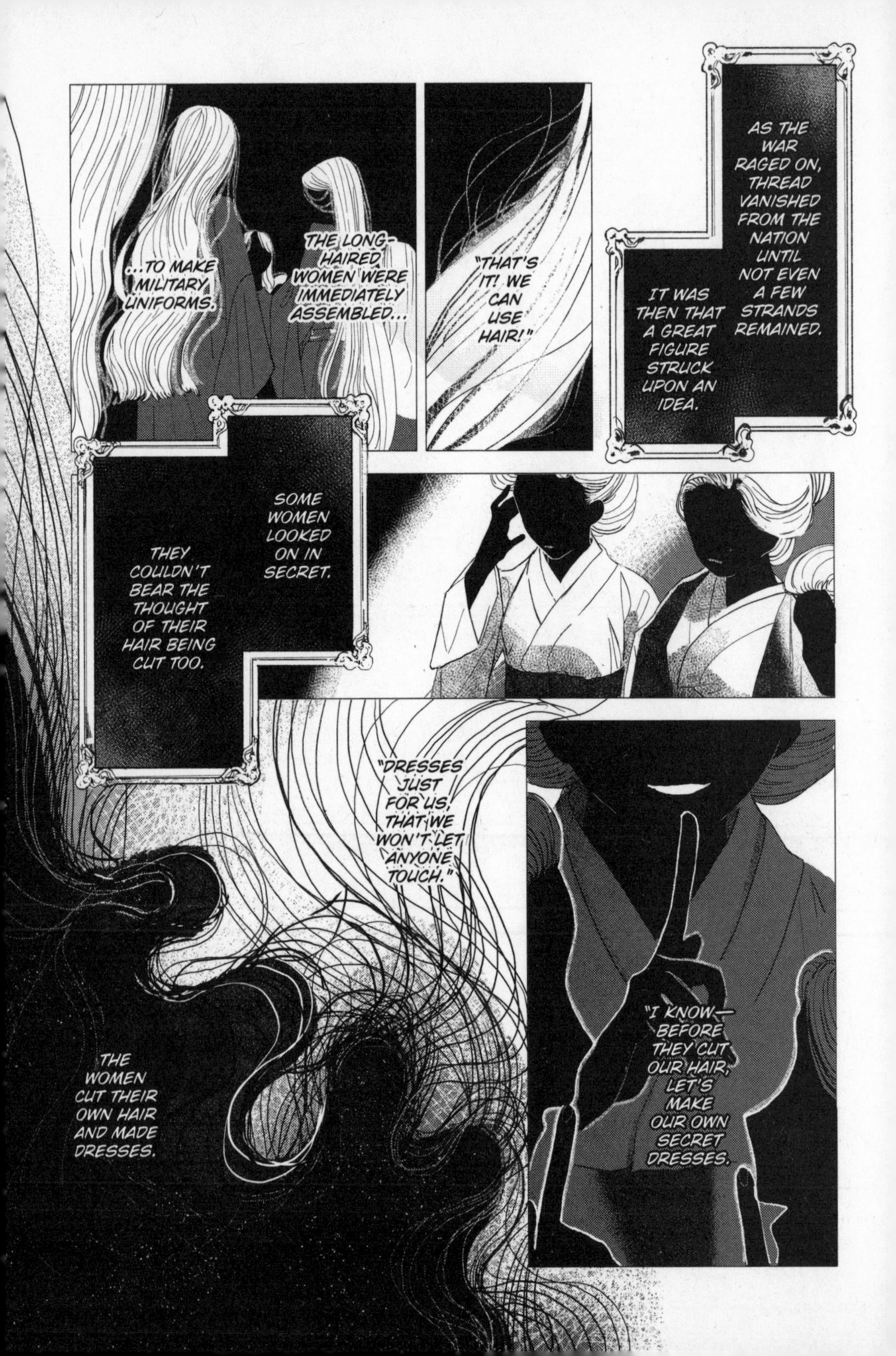
AS THE WAR RAGED ON, THREAD VANISHED FROM THE NATION UNTIL NOT EVEN A FEW STRANDS REMAINED.
IT WAS THEN THAT A GREAT FIGURE STRUCK UPON AN IDEA.
"THAT'S IT! WE CAN USE HAIR!"
THE LONG-HAIRED WOMEN WERE IMMEDIATELY ASSEMBLED...
...TO MAKE MILITARY UNIFORMS.
SOME WOMEN LOOKED ON IN SECRET.
THEY COULDN'T BEAR THE THOUGHT OF THEIR HAIR BEING CUT TOO.
"I KNOW— BEFORE THEY CUT OUR HAIR, LET'S MAKE OUR OWN SECRET DRESSES.
"DRESSES JUST FOR US, THAT WE WON'T LET ANYONE TOUCH."
THE WOMEN CUT THEIR OWN HAIR AND MADE DRESSES.

IT'S SAID THE DRESSES WERE INCREDIBLY BEAUTIFUL...
...AND THAT THOSE WHO WORE THEM ALL SAID...
..."IT'S ALMOST AS THOUGH THE DRESS IS BREATHING."
THE SECRET DRESS-MAKING AND THE WAR BOTH ENDED. NOW THEY'RE JUST STORIES OF THE PAST...

THAT SHOULD BE ENOUGH.
IT'S TRULY LOVELY.
...EXCEPT FOR ONE TRADITION.
I ENVY THE NEW STUDENT WHO WILL RECEIVE YOUR UNIFORM, ONEE-SAMA.

I'VE BEEN GOING TO THIS SCHOOL FOR SIX YEARS, AND I'M STILL NOT USED TO THE DORM'S SISTER THING.
COMMUTERS
SAME.
HAAH...

THAT'S NOTHING FOR A PRINCE TO SAY.
ERK ...
IT'S WARM FOR DECEMBER, ISN'T IT?
NO?
......YEAH.

LET'S GO.
SAY, APPARENTLY, THAT CAKE SHOP TWO STOPS AWAY HAS THESE NEW SHIBA INU MACARONS.
HUH !?
WANT TO GO?
YEAH !!
ZA (WHOOSH)
EEEEK!

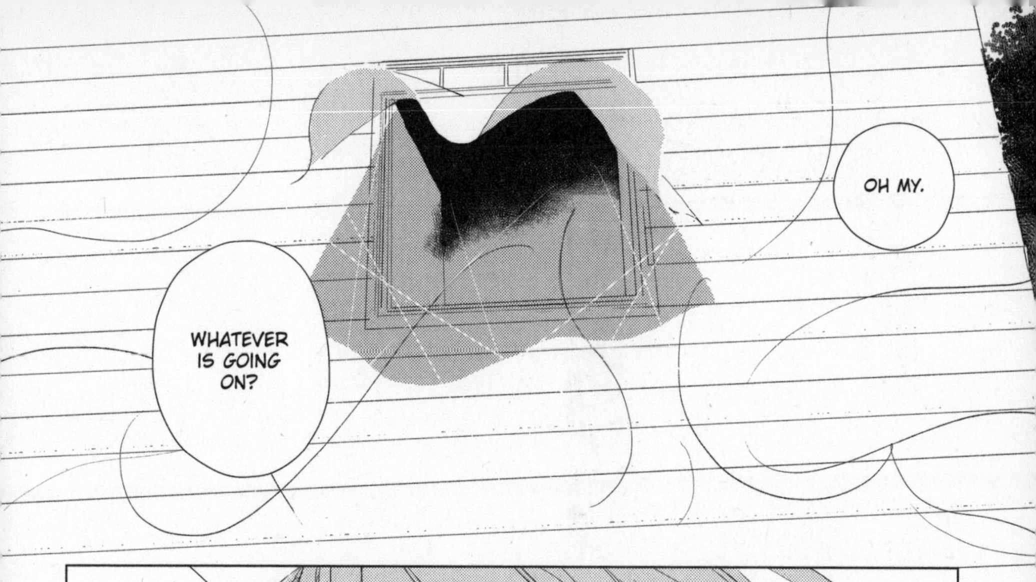
OH MY.
WHATEVER IS GOING ON?

JUST NOW...FROM HOSHIMIYA-SAN'S ROOM......

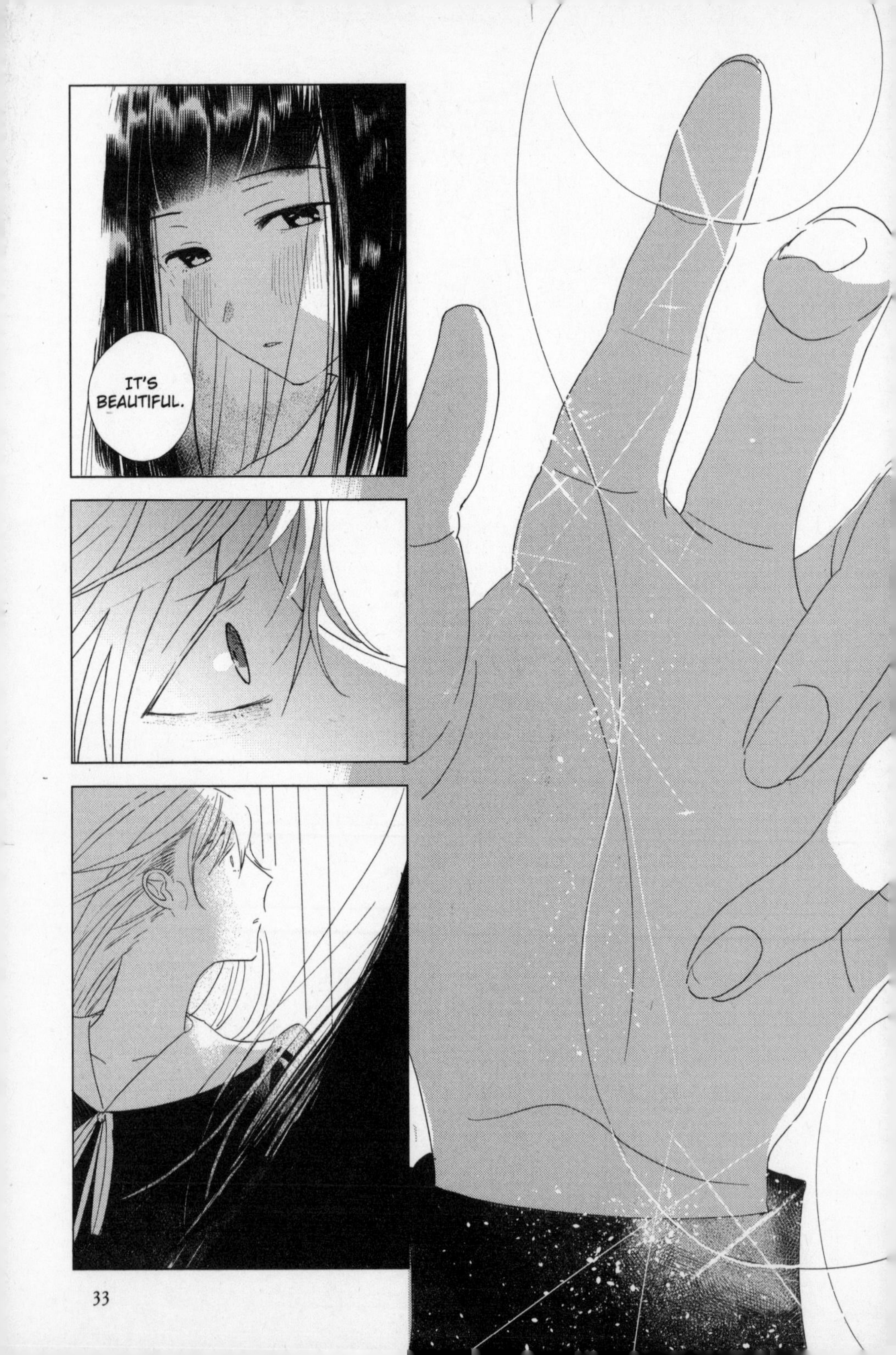
IT'S BEAUTIFUL.

OUR UNIFORMS ARE MADE OF HAIR.

Cocoon Entwined

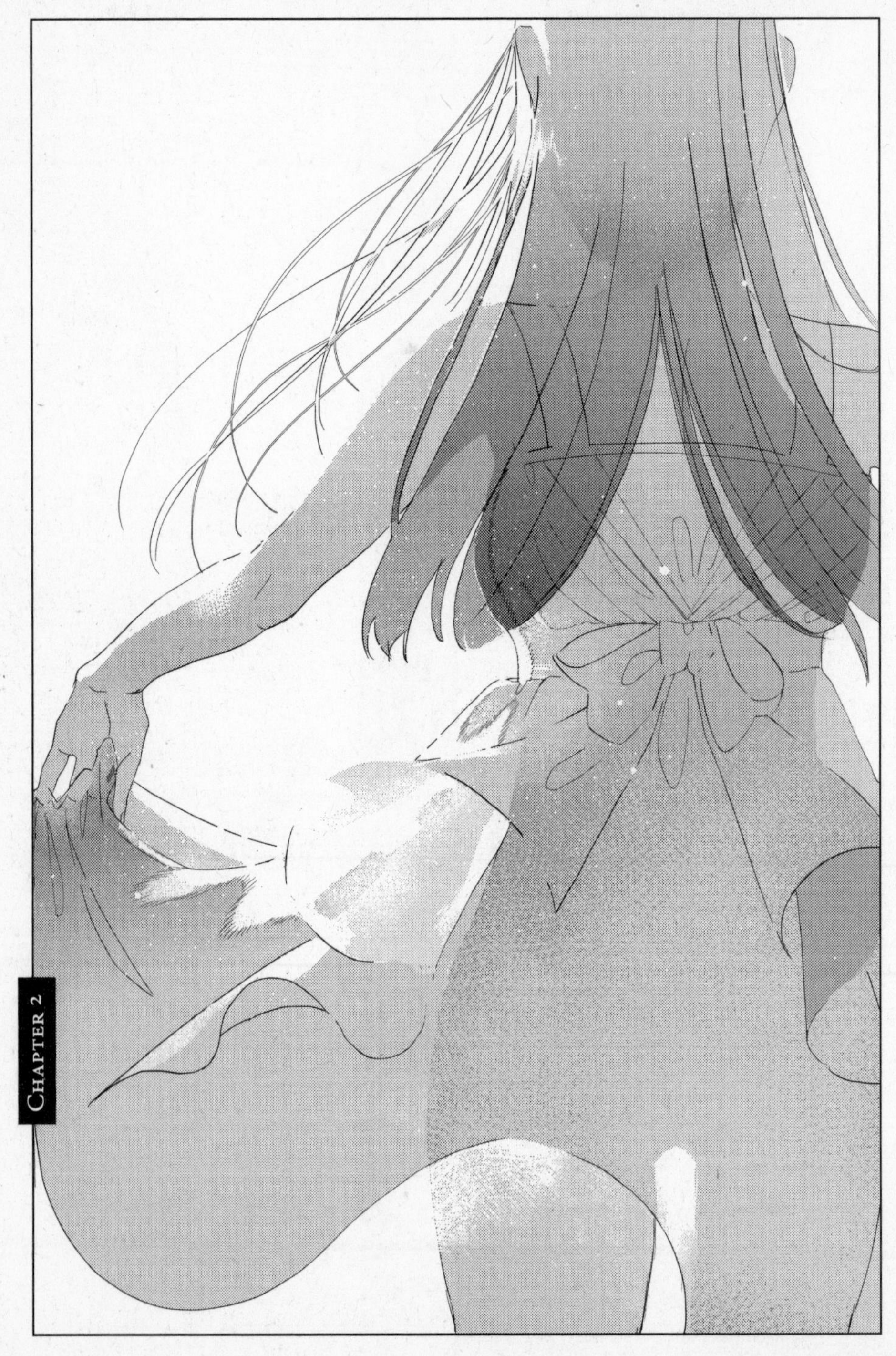

SHOULDER WIDTH— THIRTY-SIX.
HIPS— EIGHTY.
SLEEVE LENGTH— FIFTY-TWO.
WAIST— FIFTY-NINE.
BUST— EIGHTY.

HEAD— FIFTY-ONE.
THIS IS REALLY VULGAR, ISN'T IT?
TOTALLY.
I WON'T LISTEN WHEN IT'S YOUR TURN, MIIKO.
REALLY?
OH YEAH, WHERE'S HOSHIMIYA-SAN?
IT SEEMS LIKE SHE'S IN A SEPARATE ROOM.
LUCKY!
MIDDLE SCHOOL DIVISION THIRD-YEAR YOUKO YOKOZAWA

THEY'RE DOING THE HIGH SCHOOL THIRD-YEARS' HAIRCUTTING CEREMONY ON THE SECOND FLOOR, AREN'T THEY?
I WONDER WHAT THAT MUST BE LIKE.
RIGHT?
YOU REALLY HAVE TO WONDER.
JUST BETWEEN US...
...I HEARD IF YOUR HAIR ISN'T LONG ENOUGH, THEY'LL SEND YOU HOME WITHOUT CUTTING IT.
REALLY? YOU'RE DISQUALIFIED?
PROBABLY BECAUSE THERE WOULDN'T BE ENOUGH TO MAKE A UNIFORM.
WILL I HAVE ENOUGH? I'VE ONLY BEEN GROWING MINE OUT SINCE SECOND GRADE.
YOKOZAWA-SAN, RIGHT?

OUR TURNS SURE ARE TAKING A WHILE TO COME, AREN'T THEY?

HUH?

YES, IT SEEMS SO...
YOU DON'T NEED TO BE FORMAL WITH ME.

SAEKI-SAN'S IS LONGER THAN MINE.
YOU KNOW, I'VE BEEN THINKING THIS FOR A WHILE...

...BUT YOU HAVE SUCH PRETTY HAIR, YOKOZAWA-SAN.

THAT'S NOT NICE.
BEING TEASED...
...OVER MY HAIR LIKE THAT ISN'T NICE.
PLUS, UNLIKE ALL THE OTHER GIRLS WHO'VE BEEN GROWING THEIR HAIR OUT SINCE FOREVER, I'VE ONLY BEEN GROWING MINE OUT SINCE SIXTH GRADE.
I CAN'T AFFORD EXPENSIVE STUFF LIKE HAIR TREATMENT.
NO ONE...
I DON'T WANT TO SAY THESE THINGS.
...WOULD WANT MY UNI—

DON'T SAY THAT.
SU (BRUSH)
YOUR HAIR IS SO SILKY...
...AND SO DELICATE, IT SEEMS LIKE IT COULD BREAK AT THE SLIGHTEST TOUCH.
I THINK IT'S GOING TO MAKE A REALLY LOVELY UNIFORM.

PRETTY HAIR?
THAT WAS EMPTY FLATTERY, HANDS DOWN.
BUT...

I'D BETTER HURRY BACK.
SNOW.
ON THE LAST DAY OF WINTER BREAK...
...THE HIGH SCHOOL THIRD-YEARS AND MIDDLE SCHOOL THIRD-YEARS ARE ASSEMBLED IN THE DRESSMAKING BUILDING.
THE MIDDLE SCHOOLERS FOR UNIFORM MEASUREMENTS...

...AND THE HIGH SCHOOLERS FOR...

NNNNGH!
BATAN (SLAM)
THE TEACHERS NEVER SAID WE COULDN'T...... BUT...
JUST... JUST A QUICK PEEK...

PETAN (PLOP)
KON (KNOCK)
PARDON ME.
KON
KYU (SQUEAK)
CLASS 3-A, SAKI MAEZONO.
SU (SWISH)
I'M READY.

COULD YOU PLEASE WAIT A MOMENT?
I'M SORRY.

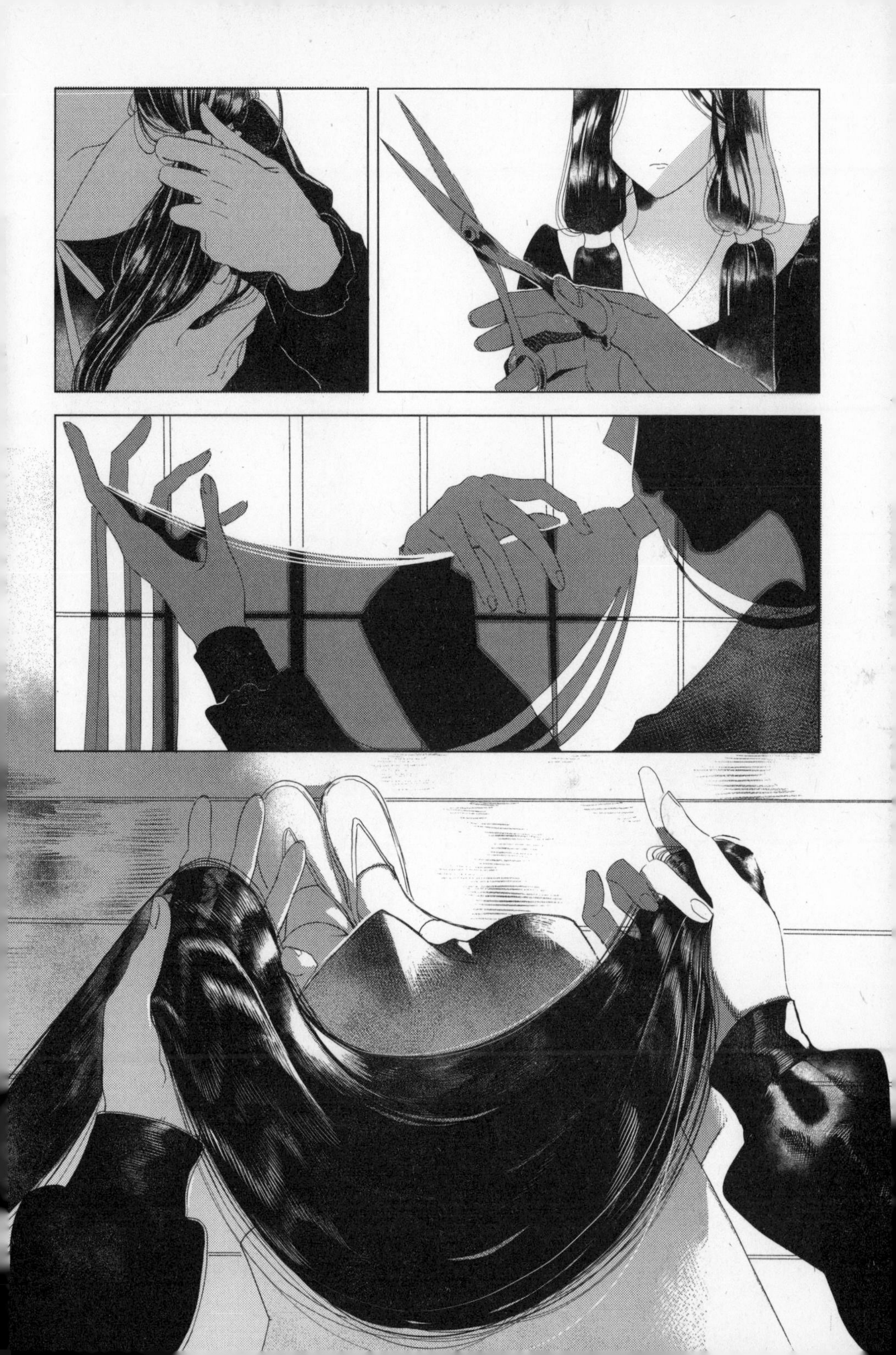

THANK YOU FOR EVERYTHING.
KON (KNOCK)
KON
PARDON ME.

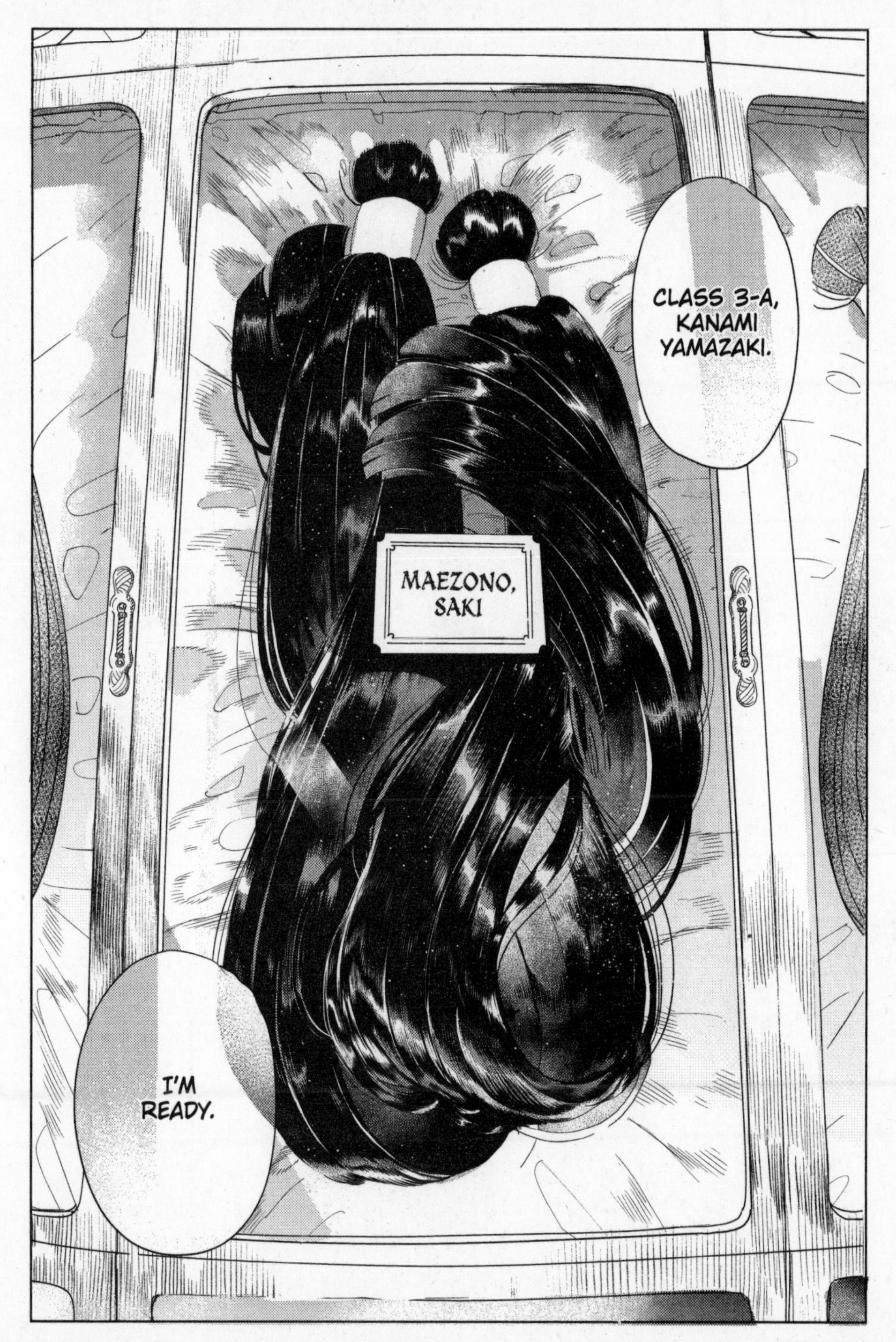
CLASS 3-A, KANAMI YAMAZAKI.
MAEZONO, SAKI
I'M READY.

Cocoon Entwined

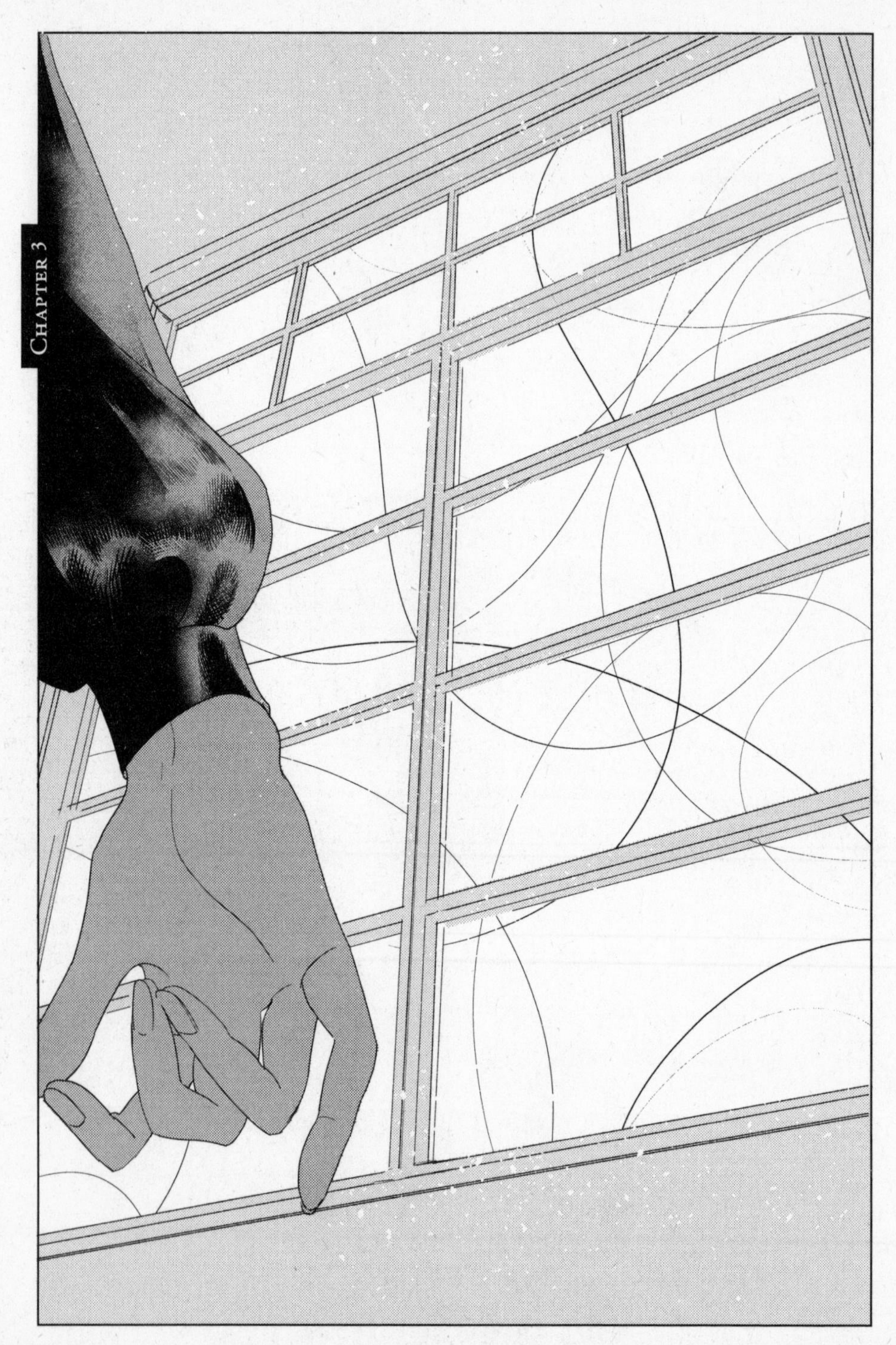

HIGH SCHOOL DIVISION THIRD-YEAR YUKA HANYUU
I KNEW RIGHT AWAY THAT IT BELONGED TO HOSHIMIYA-SAN.
I SPOKE TO HER BEFORE— JUST ONCE.

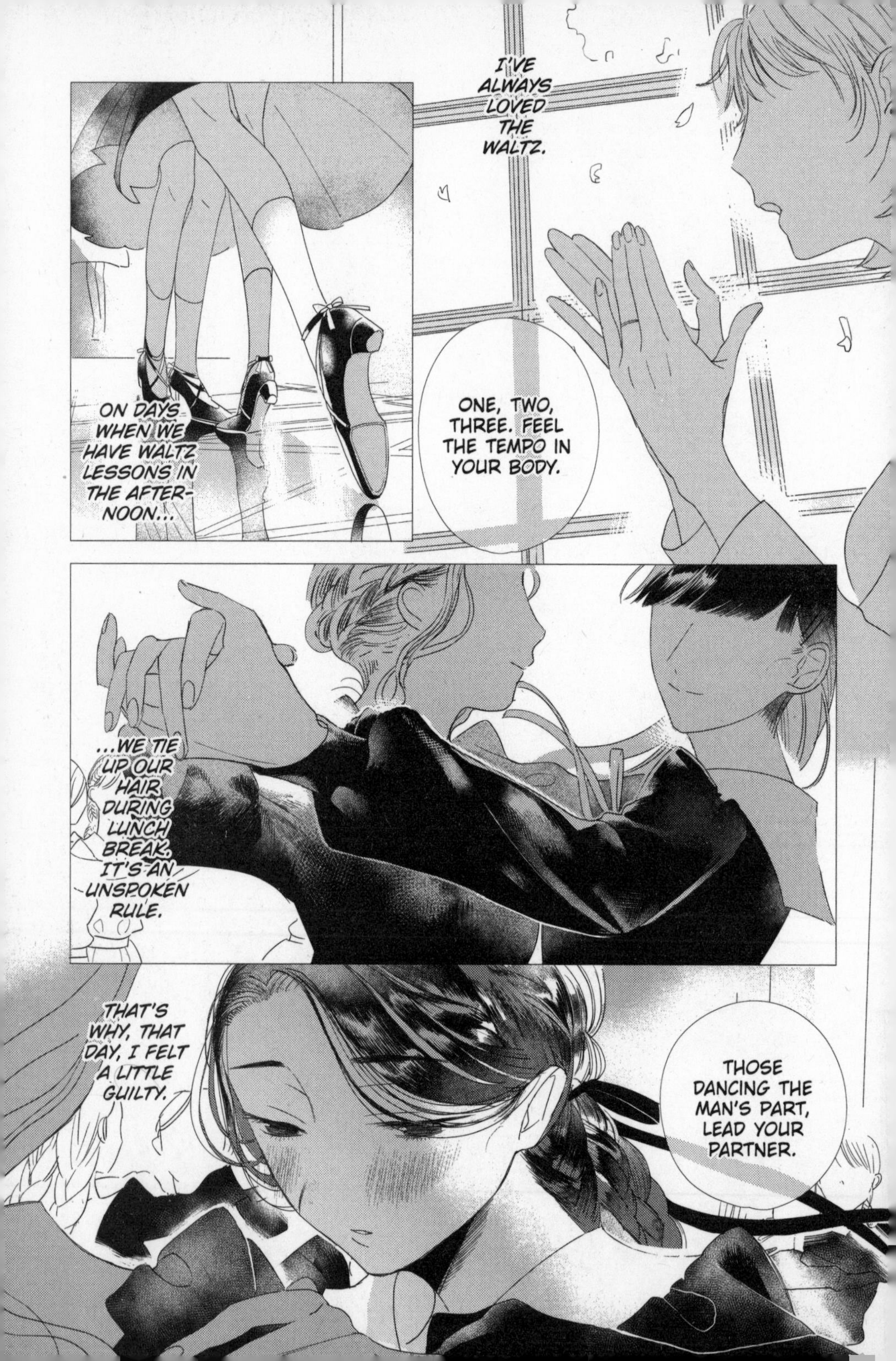
I'VE ALWAYS LOVED THE WALTZ.
ONE, TWO, THREE. FEEL THE TEMPO IN YOUR BODY.
ON DAYS WHEN WE HAVE WALTZ LESSONS IN THE AFTER-NOON...
...WE TIE UP OUR HAIR DURING LUNCH BREAK. IT'S AN UNSPOKEN RULE.
THOSE DANCING THE MAN'S PART, LEAD YOUR PARTNER.
THAT'S WHY, THAT DAY, I FELT A LITTLE GUILTY.

BECAUSE, EVEN THOUGH I ADORED THE GIRLS DANCING WITH THEIR LONG HAIR NEATLY GATHERED UP...
NATURAL TURN.

...AND THE PERFECT HARMONY OF THE WALTZ...
REVERSE TURN.
...I COULDN'T HELP BUT BE MESMERIZED...

...BY HOSHIMIYA-SAN'S HAIR.
SHE FLOATED IN THE MIDST OF THE WALTZ, SO VERY FREE...
...AND LUSTROUS.

HEY.
WHY DO YOU TRY TO TIE UP YOUR HAIR?
DANCE WITH ME LIKE THAT.

HANYUU-SAN?

WE'LL HELP YOU TIE UP YOUR HAIR.
THANK YOU FOR ALWAYS DOING THIS.
IT'S NO PROBLEM. DON'T WORRY ABOUT IT.
THAT REMINDS ME. HOSHIMIYA-SAN...
PIKU (TWITCH)
WHY DOESN'T SHE TIE UP HER HAIR?
I KNOW! I WAS SO SCARED OF ACCIDENTALLY STEPPING ON IT.
IT WOULD BE SO MUCH BETTER TO TIE IT UP, WOULDN'T IT?

I DON'T THINK SO......

AH!

YOU'RE RIGHT. IT'S SO BEAUTIFUL. IT WOULD BE A TERRIBLE SHAME IF IT CAUGHT ON SOMETHING AND HAD TO BE CUT.
RIGHT? EXACTLY.
PA (POP)

I KNOW!
WHY DON'T WE GO BUY A BARRETTE OR SCRUNCHIE THAT WOULD SUIT HOSHIMIYA-SAN?

SO (SLIP)
WELL, HANYUU-SAN...?
...WHAT DO YOU THINK?
YES.
ON OUR NEXT DAY OFF, WE'LL GET PERMISSION TO GO OUT AND BUY ONE.
A HAIR TIE THAT WOULD SUIT HOSHIMIYA-SAN......

I DO RECALL ...
... HOSHIMIYA-SAN'S ROOM WAS ON THE TOP FLOOR AT THE END OF THE HALL...
BA CTURN
HOSHI-MIYA...
... SAN?

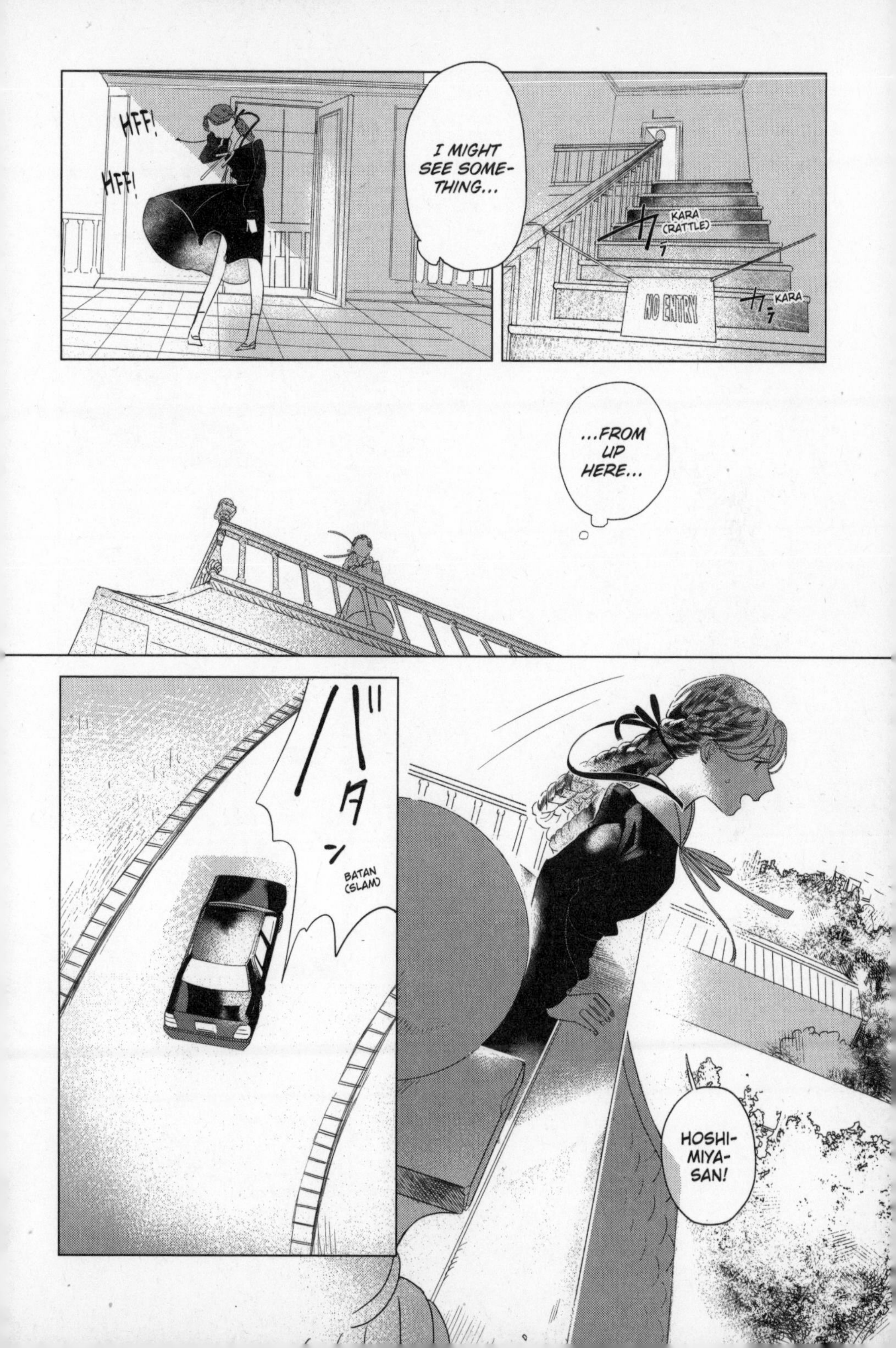
KARA (RATTLE)
KARA
NO ENTRY
I MIGHT SEE SOME-THING...
HFF!
HFF!
...FROM UP HERE...
HOSHI-MIYA-SAN!
BATAN (SLAM)

HOSHI-
MIYA-
SAN!
HOSHI-
MIYA-
SAN!
BURORO (VROOM)
DANCE WITH ME LIKE THAT.

WHAT WOULD HAPPEN IF WE RUINED THIS WALTZ?

PFFT!
HA-HA!

AH
HA
HA!

...REVIVED.
AHH...I FEEL THE SLIGHTEST BIT...

Cocoon Entwined

SAEKI-SAN.
HAVE YOU GOTTEN TALLER AGAIN?
HAVE I?
YOU'RE WEARING A COAT SO SOON? HAVE YOU COME DOWN WITH A COLD, PERHAPS?
SAEKI-SAN, I BAKED THESE COOKIES FOR YOU. WOULD YOU—?
LATER, OKAY?
HIGH SCHOOL DIVISION FIRST-YEAR HANA SAEKI
HEY, SAEKI-SAN.
SORRY, LADIES. I'M AFRAID I'M IN A BIT OF A HURRY.
PA (FWIP)
AND I WAS SO SURE I'D GET HER TO ACCEPT MY COOKIES TODAY!
SHE OBVIOUSLY CAN'T ACCEPT PERSONAL GIFTS.

AFTER ALL, THE PRINCE BELONGS TO EVERYONE.
CHAPTER 4

I'M SORRY I'M LATE.
IT'S FINE.
PRINCES ALWAYS MAKE A LATE ENTRANCE.
YOU HAVEN'T BEEN IN THE DRESSMAKING BUILDING SINCE YOU WERE MEASURED, RIGHT?
YES.
ARE YOU KEEPING UP ALL RIGHT WITH HIGH SCHOOL CLASSES?
YES, I'M MANAGING.

GII (CREAK)
THIS IS KIND OF LIKE...
...A CATA-COMB, ISN'T IT?
OH, THOSE UNDERGROUND TOMBS? I'M IMPRESSED YOU KNOW WHAT THOSE ARE.
I'LL GET THE LIGHT. YOU WAIT THERE.

THE TOMB OF THE DRESSMAKING BUILDING, HMM? I LIKE THAT.

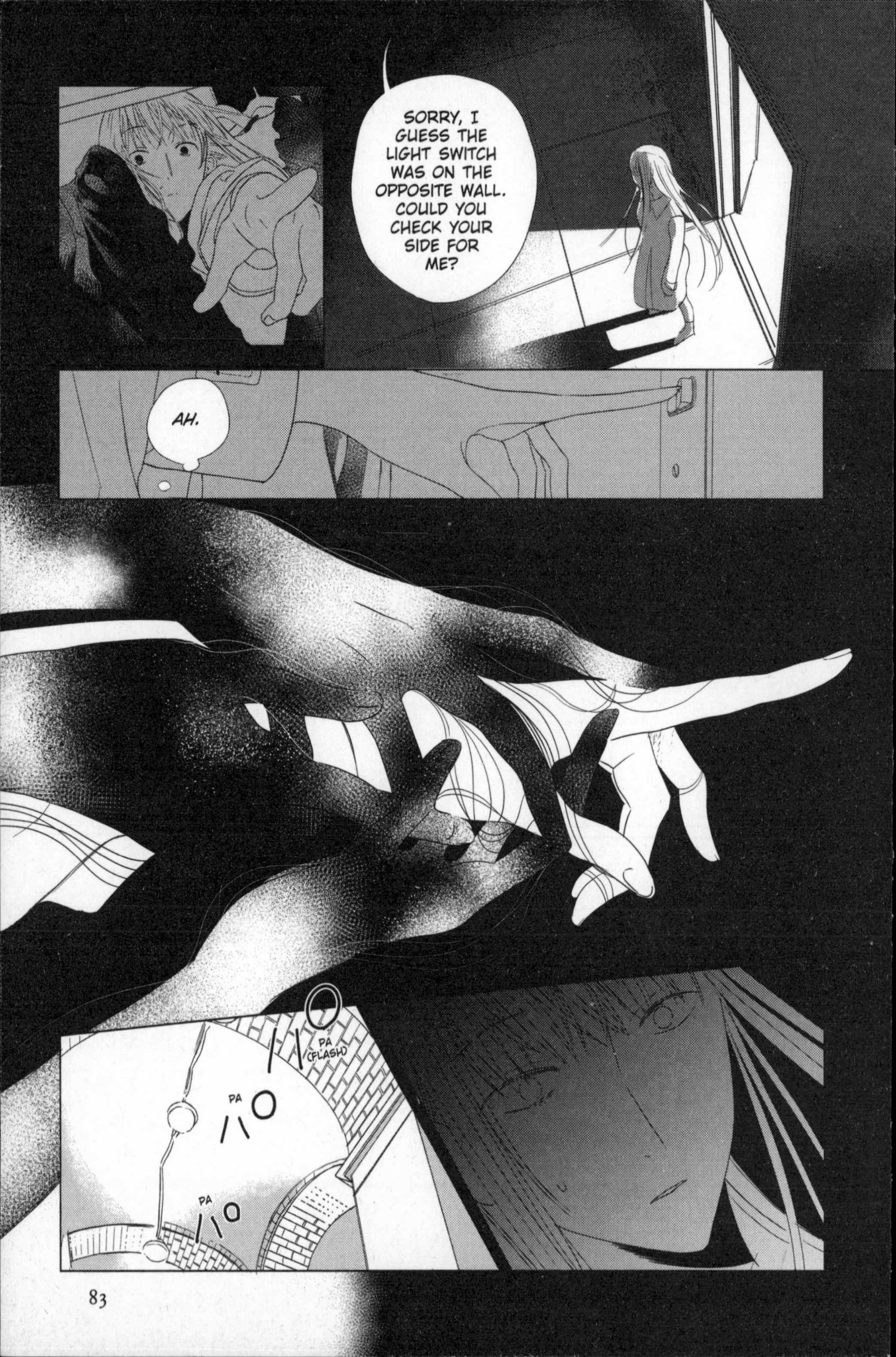
SORRY, I GUESS THE LIGHT SWITCH WAS ON THE OPPOSITE WALL. COULD YOU CHECK YOUR SIDE FOR ME?
AH.
PA (FLASH)
PA
PA

PA (FLASH)
KARARA (RATTLE)
SOMETHING WRONG?
IT FELT LIKE SOMEONE TOUCHED ME......
THE UNIFORMS LEFT BEHIND BY OUR ALUMNI ARE LOCKED UP HERE...
...FOR DECADES, AFTER ALL.
MAYBE THE THOUGHT OF BEING WORN AGAIN GOT THEM EXCITED.
AND THE CHANCE OF BEING CHOSEN BY A PRINCE, AT THAT.

YOU CAN TAKE YOUR UNIFORM WITH YOU WHEN YOU GRADUATE, BUT SOME GIRLS LEAVE THEIRS TOO.
I DIDN'T KNOW ABOUT THIS PLACE UNTIL AFTER I BECAME A TEACHER MYSELF.
ANY-WAY...
...WE OPENED THIS TOMB UP FOR YOU, SO GET READY.
AH...
MY, MY...
IT'S WORSE THAN I HEARD ...
YOU'VE REALLY SHOT UP, HAVEN'T YOU......?
I HOPE I CAN FIND A UNIFORM THAT FITS.

IS SOME-THING THE MATTER?
?
NO, I WAS JUST THINKING... I CAN UNDERSTAND HOW THESE UNIFORMS FEEL.
MM-HM.

HMM...
NOT HERE EITHER......

UMM...
I HATE TO BE THE BEARER OF BAD NEWS, BUT...

NONE OF THESE UNIFORMS FIT YOUR HEIGHT.

I SPOKE TO HIYAMA-SENSEI, THE DRESSMAKING TEACHER...... AND IT SOUNDS LIKE, IF THERE'S NOTHING HERE...
...ALL WE CAN DO IS ADD TO THE UNIFORM YOU HAVE NOW WITH ORDINARY FABRIC......
I UNDERSTAND.

THAT'S FINE WITH ME.
HMM...NOW THAT THAT'S SETTLED, WHAT SHOULD WE HAVE YOU DO IN THE MEANTIME?
I DON'T MIND GOING TO SCHOOL IN A TRACKSUIT FOR A LITTLE WHILE.
YOU KNOW THAT WON'T FLY.
COME TO THINK OF IT...

WHY DID YOU ENROLL IN THIS SCHOOL, SAEKI-SAN?
ME?
MY MOM SAID SHE WAS DEAD SET ON SENDING HER DAUGHTER HERE IF SHE HAD ONE...
...BUT HER FIRST TWO KIDS WERE BOYS.
OHHH, I TOTALLY GET IT. THIS SCHOOL'S PRETTY POPULAR WITH THE MOMS.
THOUGH, I BET IT'D NEVER EVEN OCCUR TO MOM THAT I'M PUTTING ON THIS BOY ACT HERE......
DON (BUMP)
WHOA, THERE.
MY BAD. I WASN'T PAYING ATTENTION.

IF ANYTHING HAPPENED TO YOUR HAIR...
IT'S FINE.
YOU SURE YOU'RE ALL RIGHT? YOU'RE NOT HURT?

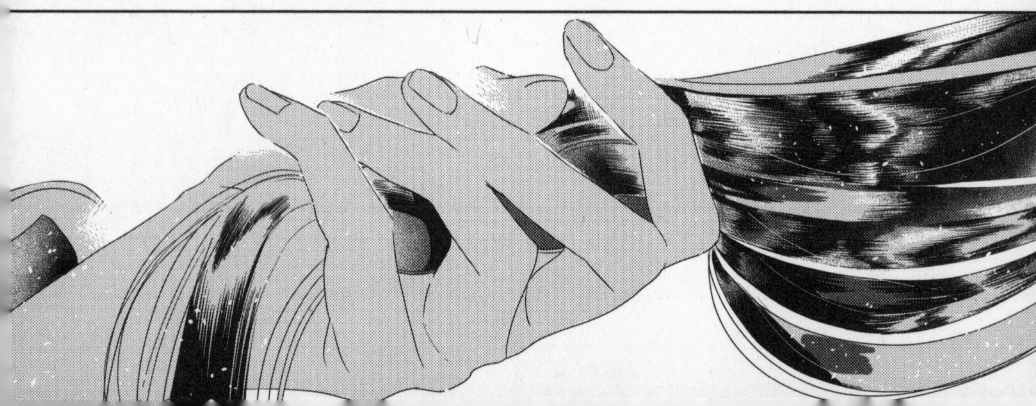

I CAN ASSURE YOU I'M QUITE FINE.

WAS THAT GIRL...

...
HOSHIMIYA-SAN?
HER HAIR WAS INCREDIBLY LIGHT......
SO LIGHT......
...TO THE POINT WHERE IT COULD JUST FLY OFF.
AHH...

IT'S EXHAUSTING ...

IF ONLY THIS UNIFORM WOULD JUST FLY AWAY AND DISAPPEAR TOO—

Cocoon Entwined

I LOOK LIKE MY GOOD-LOOKING OLDER BROTHER, SO EVER SINCE MIDDLE SCHOOL, I'VE SOMEHOW ENDED UP PLAYING THAT KIND OF ROLE.
PEOPLE OFTEN SAID, "SAEKI-SAN IS SO COOL, ISN'T SHE?"
I DIDN'T DISLIKE HEARING THAT. AS LONG AS I COULD ENJOY AN EASY SCHOOL LIFE, IT DIDN'T MATTER TO ME.

BUT AFTER I SLIPPED INTO THIS UNIFORM, THE WAY EVERYONE LOOKED AT ME CHANGED.
"PRINCE."
AFTER SOMEONE LET THAT WORD OUT, IT QUICKLY BECAME SYNONYMOUS WITH ME.
IT'S ALMOST...

...AS IF THIS UNIFORM TRANSFORMS ME INTO A PRINCE.

UH?
NNGH...
SIX O' CLOCK ...
TIME TO HEAD HOME.
THOSE FANGIRLS NEVER LEARN, DO THEY?
SURELY, NONE OF THEM WOULD WAIT AROUND THIS LONG...
HOW WAS SCHOOL TODAY?
COME ON!-DID SOMETHING HAPPEN? TELL ME!!
...BUT IT'S A PAIN IN THE NECK TO GO STRAIGHT HOME AND HAVE MOM GRILL ME ABOUT SCHOOL...

THAT WINDOW BELONGS TO THE GIRL FROM YESTERDAY ......
TO HOSHIMIYA-SAN.

WHA—!?
DA (DASH)
WHAT IS SHE THINKING !?

WHOA!
OW, OW, OW...
HOWEVER LIGHT YOU MAY BE, YOU CAN'T FLY THROUGH THE SKY.
TRUE.
I COULDN'T FLY.
IS SHE A LITTLE NUTTY...?
NOT THAT I SHOULD TALK ....
YOU'RE NOT HURT?
YOU'RE OKAY?

I HAD THIS FEELING AS THOUGH I COULD RUN FAR, FAR AWAY.

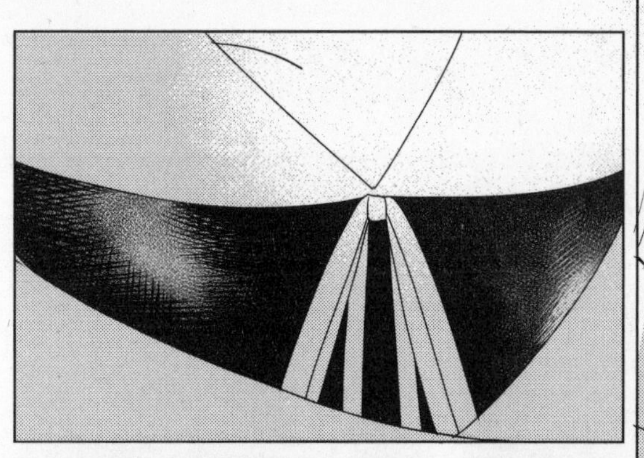

THEN...

...WANNA RUN AWAY FROM HERE WITH ME?
HEY, LOOK!

AREN'T THOSE HOSHIMIYA ACADEMY STUDENTS?
WHAT? NO WAY! YOU'RE RIGHT!
I'VE ONLY SEEN THEM ON TV. THEIR HAIR REALLY IS LONG.
NIKO (GRIN)
SHE JUST SMILED AT US!!
WE'VE BEEN RIDING THE TRAIN FOR AN HOUR AND A HALF......
CHIRA (GLANCE)
CHIRA
SO THIS IS THE GENERAL REACTION WE GET, HUH...?
WHO WOULD'VE THOUGHT HOSHIMIYA-SAN WOULD ACTUALLY COME WITH ME...?

SHE SITS NEXT TO THE HEAD-MISTRESS DURING EVENTS LIKE ASSEMBLIES ...

SMALL, WITH LONG EYELASHES AND LONG HAIR.

I ALWAYS THOUGHT SHE WAS JUST A PRETTY DOLL.

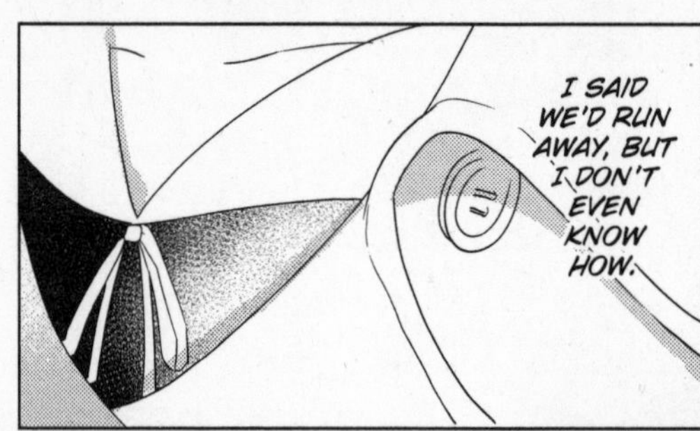
I SAID WE'D RUN AWAY, BUT I DON'T EVEN KNOW HOW.

BUT THE SAME GOES FOR ME...

...I THOUGHT THIS MIGHT LEAD TO SOMETHING...
BUT...

...AND GOT MY HOPES UP A LITTLE......
PACIFICO YOKOHAMA
ONCE WE REACHED THE LAST STOP...
...I THOUGHT MAYBE SOME-THING WOULD CHANGE...BUT I GUESS NOT.
NOT EVEN TWO THOUSAND YEN...?
I SHOULD TELL HER WE'D BETTER GO BACK, AFTER ALL.

HEY, HOSHIMIYA-SAN.

WHAT'S THE MATTER?
ARE YOU THIRSTY? I'LL POP OVER THERE AND BUY SOMETHING.
THIS HUMBLE ESCAPE ...
THE DOWNTOWN DISTRICT I'M SICK OF SEEING...

BOTA (DRIP)
BOTA
SORRY, PAL.
SHE BELONGS TO ME.
SHALL WE, HOSHIMIYA-SAN?

HEY!

HOW CAN SHE LOOK SO EXCITED BY IT?
IT MAKES ME—THE ONE WHO WHISKED HER AWAY...
...FEEL LIKE A REAL PRINCE.
WOULD HOSHIMIYA-SAN DRINK THINGS LIKE THIS?
HEY THERE. AREN'T YOU A HOSHIMIYA GIRL?
YOU WAITING FOR SOME-BODY?
BA (FWOOP)

WHERE ARE WE GOING?
WHERE ELSE?
WE'RE GOING FARTHER ...
...AND FARTHER ...

...AWAY.
IT TRULY...

...DOES FEEL LIKE I COULD RUN FAR, FAR AWAY.

WHAT IS IT?

COMING FROM THE PRI—
NO...
COMING FROM ME...
...THIS MIGHT SOUND FAKE, BUT...
...YOU REALLY DID SEEM LIKE YOU WERE GOING TO GO OFF SOMEWHERE... THAT'S WHY I......
THEN WILL YOU TAKE ME AWAY?
TO A PLACE EVEN THE UNIFORMS WON'T REACH.

EVEN IF A PRINCE IS SOMETHING CREATED BY SOMEONE...
ALL RIGHT.
I'LL TAKE YOU—
...FOR YOU, I CAN BECOME A REAL ONE. I'M CERTAIN OF IT.
I'M SORRY ......

FORGET WHAT I SAID......
I COULDN'T RUN ANYWHERE, AFTER ALL.
YOUNG MISS.
WE LOOKED ALL OVER FOR YOU.
YOUR GRAND-MOTHER IS WORRIED SICK.
COME—LET'S GO BACK TO THE ACADEMY.
WAIT ...

YOU GO HOME TOO. BE CAREFUL ON YOUR WAY.
COME TO THINK OF IT...
...THAT UNIFORM OF YOURS—IT'S SUFFOCATING, YES?

DO YOU HAVE SCISSORS ?
YEAH...

YOUNG MISS!?

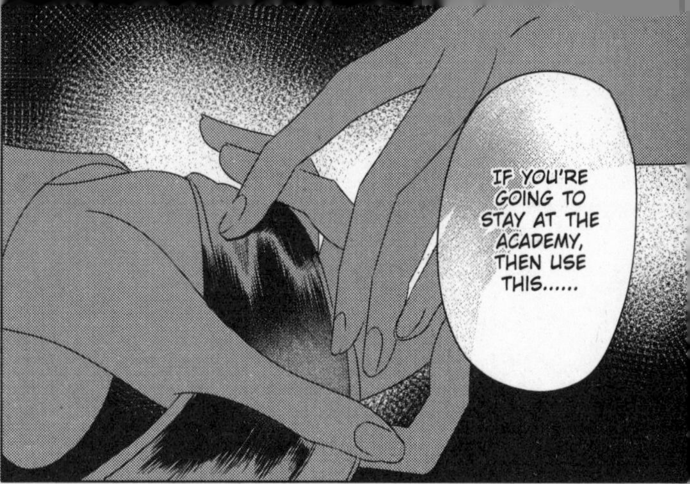
IF YOU'RE GOING TO STAY AT THE ACADEMY, THEN USE THIS......

...OR LEAVE IT. THE CHOICE IS YOURS.

GOOD NIGHT, MY PRINCE.

IT WAS A FUN DREAM.
SUU (SWISH)

OH! SAEKI-SAN! GOOD MORNING.
YOU'RE NOT WEARING A COAT!
GU (CLENCH)
YEP.

I DON'T NEED IT ANYMORE.

Cocoon Entwined

Chapter 6

OKAY, GIRLS.
THANKS FOR WIPING THE FLOORS. YOU CAN GO BACK NOW.
THANK YOU VERY MUCH FOR INSTRUCTING US!
SENPAIS.
YOUKO. WHAT ARE YOU LOOKING AT?
IF YOU DON'T DO CHORES UNTIL THE END, YOU'LL SET A BAD EXAMPLE FOR THE MIDDLE SCHOOLERS.
?
HEH HEH!
THE ROSE GARDEN? IT LOOKS BEST AROUND NOW...
I JUST FIND IT SO AMUSING.
HIGH SCHOOL DIVISION SECOND-YEAR YOUKO YOKOZAWA

IT'S SAEKI-SAN...
...HER PRECIOUS ADMIRERS, THE DORM PRINCESSES
...

...AND THEN THE FANGIRLS WHO CAN'T ENTER THEIR LITTLE CIRCLE.
THE JERK WHO PUSHED HER CLEANING ONTO ME IS ONE OF THEM.
SERVES YOU FANGIRLS RIGHT.
THEY REDID THEIR HAIR DURING CLEANING TIME FOR SAEKI-SAN...
...ONLY FOR HER TO GET SNATCHED AWAY BY THE DORM GIRLS' ELEGANT TEA PARTY. POOR THINGS!
IF THEY SLACK TOO MUCH, I'LL GIVE THEM A WARNING.
BUT ENOUGH ABOUT THEM...

INSULTS AND JEALOUSY AREN'T GOING TO GET YOU ANY OF THOSE FRIENDS YOU DON'T HAVE.
I HAVE A FRIEND OR TWO......
DOESN'T LOOK THAT WAY TO ME.
ARGH! SHUT UP!
THIS IS WHY THEY CALL YOU THE NAGGER!
I SEE.
AH!
SORRY.
YOU SHOULD BE. I CAN LET YOU GET AWAY WITH IT BECAUSE WE GREW UP TOGETHER, BUT YOU CAN'T TALK LIKE THAT TO OTHER GIRLS.

I KNOW THAT!

BUT EVERYONE'S ALREADY FOUND THEIR COCOONS. THEY'RE LIVING INSIDE THEM, STICKING TOGETHER...
LET'S LEAVE.
NO ONE WANTS A BAD TEAM PLAYER LIKE ME IN THERE...

BUT WHAT IF...

...THERE WAS SOMEONE WHO WOULD STILL ACCEPT ME...
...EVEN IF THEY KNEW THE BAD THINGS ABOUT ME?

SOME-ONE LIKE THAT...
...COULDN'T POSSIBLY...
SAEKI-SAN? IS SOMETHING THE MATTER?
I JUST SAW SOME-ONE...
OH. THE PRINCE LOOKED THIS WAY.

SHE EXISTS.
YOU HAVE SUCH PRETTY HAIR, YOKOZAWA-SAN.

THAT REMINDS ME— SAEKI-SAN.
HUH!? OH, UH, WHAT?

YOU SHOULD BE FRIENDS WITH HER.
WH-WHY?

DIDN'T YOU MENTION IT TO ME BEFORE? THAT, THE ONE TIME YOU TWO SPOKE, SHE KEPT TALKING TO YOU EVEN WHEN YOU GOT VENOMOUS.
SH-SHE SAYS THOSE THINGS TO EVERYONE. SHE'S JUST BEING NICE.

YEAH, THAT'S PROBABLY WHAT IT WAS...
NO, THAT'S DEFINITELY ALL IT WAS...
IF SAYING THINGS SHE DOESN'T MEAN WILL LEAD PEOPLE ON, SHE'LL DO IT. THAT'S HOW SHE IS.
I BET SHE DOESN'T EVEN REMEMBER WHAT SHE SAID.
SHE'S REAL SHALLOW LIKE THAT.
IF SAYING THAT WILL MAKE YOU WANT TO CRY...
...THEN YOU DON'T HAVE TO SAY IT.
SORRY.

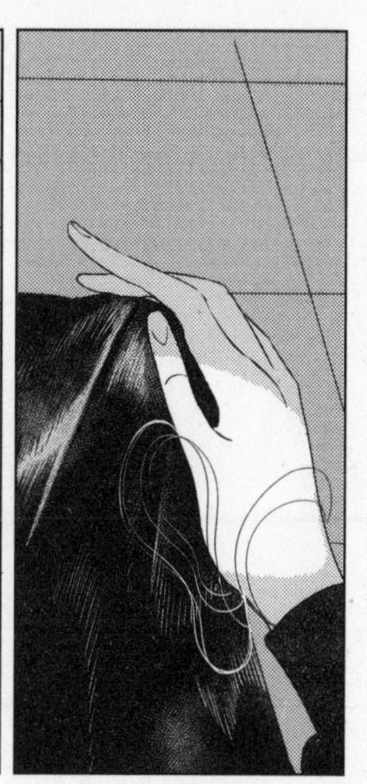

ARE YOU COMFORTING ME?

YEAH. I'M OKAY AS LONG AS I HAVE YOU.

DON'T WORRY...

...BECAUSE I WON'T WISH FOR ANYTHING MORE THAN THIS.

EXCUSE ME, GIRLS.
HAVE YOU SEEN SAEKI-SAN? I NEED HER TO COME BY THE OFFICE.
SHE'S OVER—
YOU'RE LOOKING FOR SAEKI-SAN?
YOKOZAWA-SAN SAID SHE JUST SAW HER.
HUH?
YOKOZAWA-SAN, COULD YOU GO CALL FOR HER?
I HAD A QUESTION ABOUT TODAY'S CLASSICS LESSON...
WAIT—!

Got you back.

GASA (RUSTLE)
HELLO. WHO MIGHT YOU BE?
WELL—!

OH MY. WHAT A DARLING THING. ARE YOU LOST, DEAR?
DID YOU HAVE AN INVITATION? WHAT'S YOUR NAME?
UM.
DO YOU PREFER TEA OR COFFEE?
MY MOTHER BAKED TODAY'S CAKE FROM SCRATCH. WOULD YOU CARE FOR SOME?
UH...
OR PERHAPS YOU PREFER COOKIES?
OH YES. WE WERE IN THE MIDDLE OF A DELIGHTFUL CONVERSATION.
THERE'S A SEAT OVER HERE. WON'T YOU CHAT WITH US?
I KNEW IT.
THERE'S NO WAY SHE'D REMEMBER ...

"YOKO-
ZAWA-
SAN"...
...
RIGHT?

OH
YEAH.
I ASKED
YOU TO
MEET ME
AFTER
SCHOOL
TODAY.

SORRY, I
FORGOT.

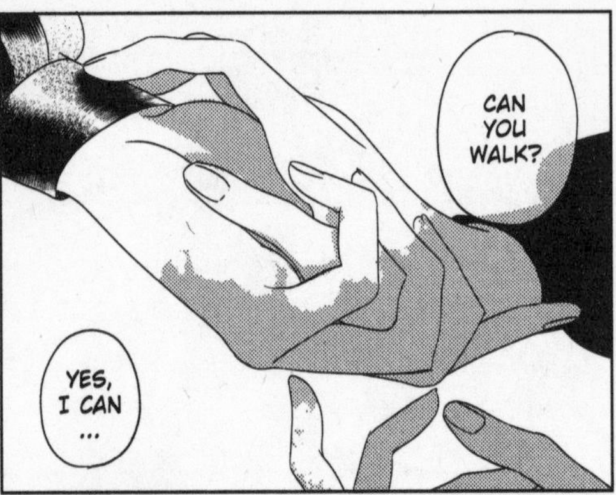
CAN YOU WALK?
YES, I CAN ...

DIDN'T I SAY YOU DIDN'T NEED TO BE SO FORMAL?
HUH?
ON MEASURING DAY.

BUT THAT...

YOU COULDN'T HAVE REMEMBERED... SOMETHING LIKE THAT......

OH, I REMEMBER IT CLEARLY.
I WANTED TO TALK TO YOU THAT DAY. THAT'S WHY I CALLED OUT TO YOU.

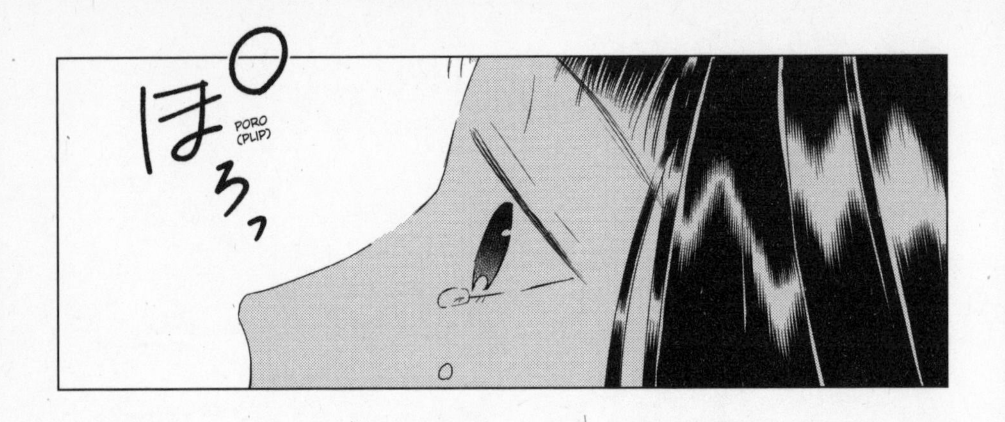

STOP.

...I'LL GET THE WRONG IDEA.

DON'T BE KIND TO ME.

Cocoon Entwined

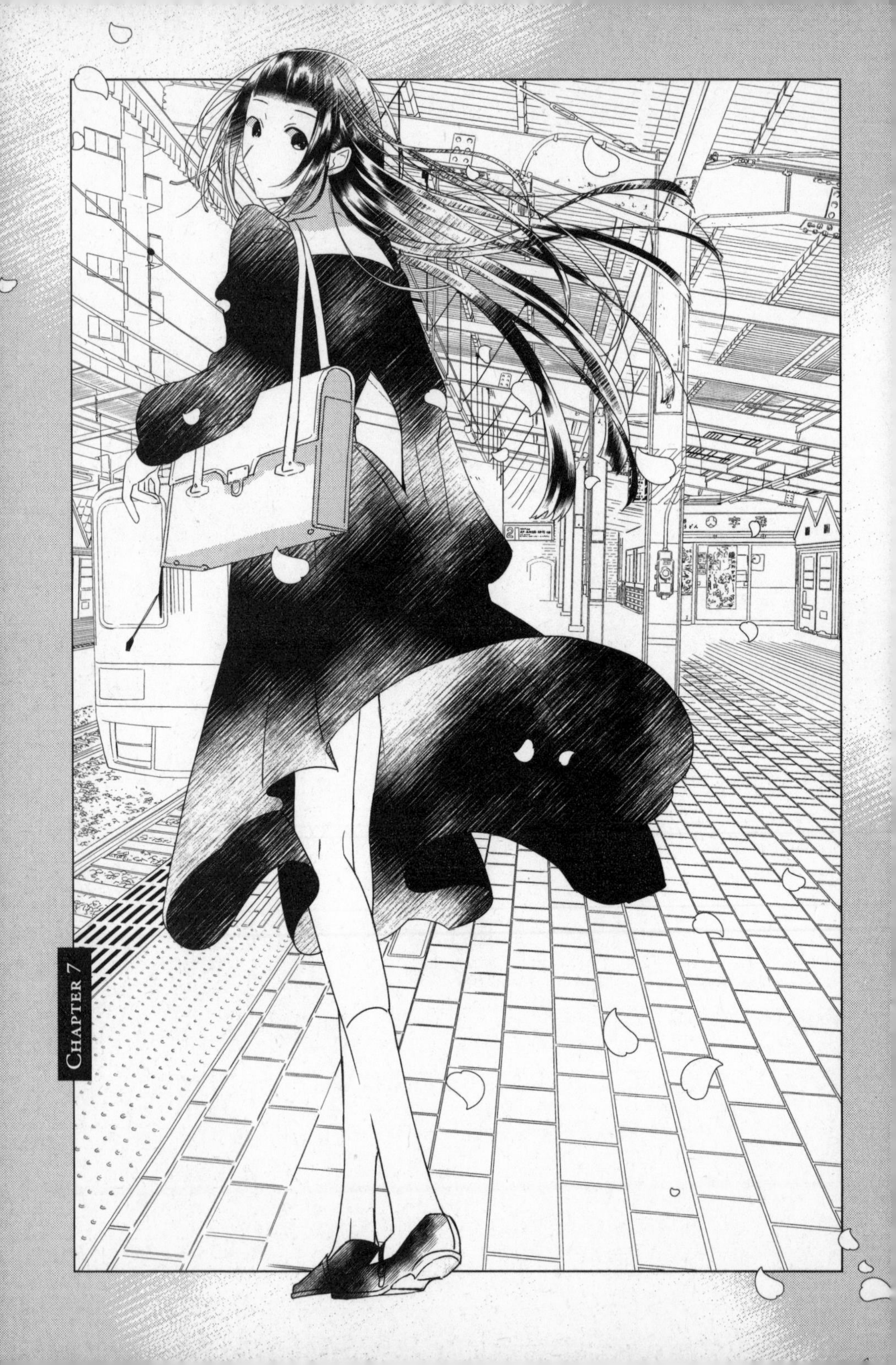
Chapter 7

SHE TOLD ME TO WAIT IN THE DRESSMAKING BUILDING...
GOD...
I DIDN'T THINK SHE REMEMBERED...

ONE WEEK AFTER THE HIGH SCHOOL ENTRANCE CEREMONY—
ARGH, COME ON!
THERE ISN'T A SINGLE GRAB HANDLE LEFT...
WHY IS IT SO CROWDED IN THE SPRING ...?
THIS SUCKS. JUST GETTING TO SCHOOL IS GONNA WIPE ME OUT...

SAEKI-SAN...!

N-NO WAY...!
SHE'S NEVER ON THE TRAIN AT THIS TIME...

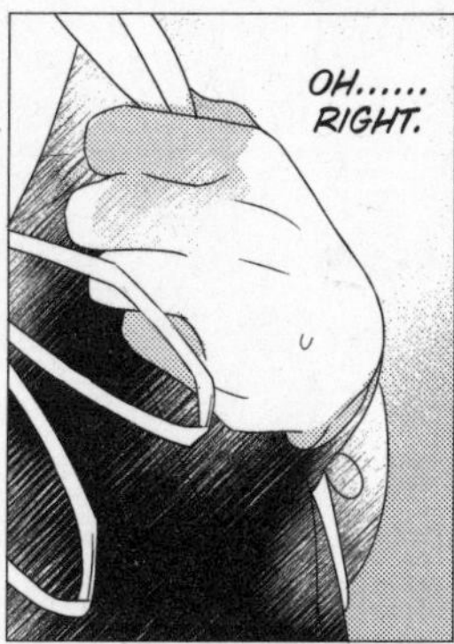
OH...... RIGHT.

YOU'D NORMALLY SAY HI...
...IN THESE SITUATIONS, RIGHT...?

WE DID TECHNICALLY START TALKING ON MEASURING DAY...IT'LL BE FI—

SHE WAS JUST BEING NICE.

... RIGHT...... THAT'S OBVIOUSLY ALL IT WAS.
I ALMOST GOT AHEAD OF MYSELF ......

GI (CREAK)
I SHOULD GET AWAY FROM HERE BEFORE SHE SEES ME......
The train...

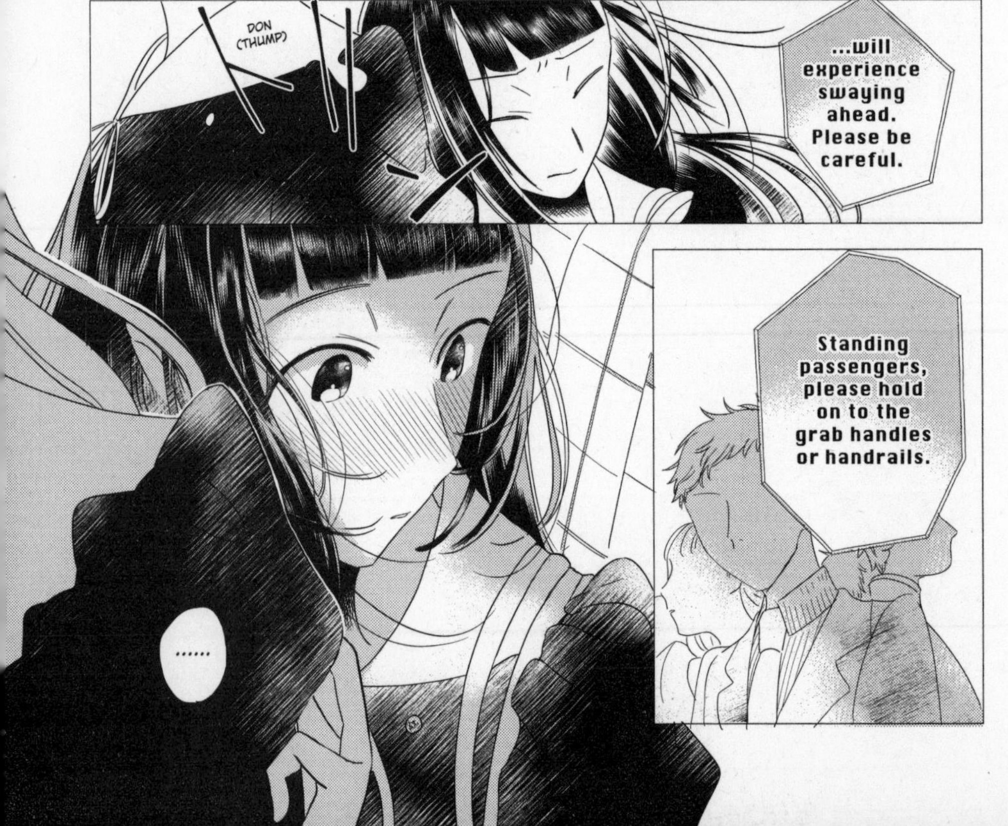

...will experience swaying ahead. Please be careful.
DON (THUMP)
Standing passengers, please hold on to the grab handles or handrails.
......

ぱ
PA (RELEASE)
......I'M SORRY.
YOU'RE FINE.

MY HAIR... LOOKS FINE...
AND MY SHOES AND BAG ARE FRESHLY POLISHED TOO...
Next stop is Hoshimiya Girls' Academy.
BUT...
...IF SHE REALLY DOES REMEMBER ...

I KNEW ALREADY.
THERE'S NO WAY SHE'D REMEMBER.
BUT I'M ALSO A LITTLE RELIEVED...
BECAUSE NOW...
...I DON'T HAVE TO GET HURT FROM GETTING INVOLVED WITH SOMEONE.
THAT'S WHY......

HERE.
I WET IT A LITTLE. YOU SHOULD COOL YOUR EYES.
I DON'T NEED YOUR ...
AH!
YOU CAN'T TALK LIKE THAT TO OTHER GIRLS.
TH...
THANKS.

OH, I SHOULD BE THANKING YOU.
I WAS SORT OF HOPING FOR AN EXCUSE TO SLIP AWAY...
...SO I WAS HAPPY WHEN YOU SHOWED UP FOR ME.
I...I DID AS I WAS ASKED... THAT'S ALL...
MOREOVER ...

...WHY THE DRESSMAKING BUILDING?
AH. THAT'S...
...'COS OF THESE.

IF MY OUTSIDE SHOES OR SCHOOLBAG ARE STILL AT SCHOOL, THE FANGIRLS WILL LOOK FOR ME, RIGHT? SOMETIMES, I HIDE MY THINGS IN HERE TO THROW THEM OFF THE SCENT.
FRANKLY, IT'S TIRING.

BY THE WAY, WHY DID YOU SAY SOMETHING ABOUT NOT REMEMBERING BACK THERE?
HUH?
W—
WELL...
......A LITTLE WHILE AFTER THE ENTRANCE CEREMONY, WE ENDED UP...... ON THE SAME TRAIN...
I WAS... REALLY CLOSE TO YOU, BUT YOU...DIDN'T NOTICE ME, SO I THOUGHT...
WHAT, THAT'S ALL?

YOU SHOULD'VE SAID SOMETHING!
IT'S NOT LIKE I WAS FAR AWAY, RIGHT?
FOR ME, IT'S A HUGE PROBLEM!
IT'S NOT THAT HARD!
THAT'S WHAT YOU THINK.

SHOOT......
I BLURTED
IT OUT......

HA HA HA!
YOU REALLY ARE ONE OF A KIND, YOKOZAWA-SAN.
IF I OFFENDED YOU, I APOLOGIZE.
HAAH...
ONE OF A KIND? WHAT'S THAT SUPPOSED TO...?
SORRY... THAT TEA PARTY LEFT ME BEAT... I CAN'T ANYMORE...
HUH!?

...HEY!
SU
(DOZE)
SHE'S
ASLEEP...
WAIT...

SHE'S CLOSE...!
HUH? WHAT DO PEOPLE DO IN SITUATIONS LIKE THIS...? AH...I... I KNOW.
HEY, YOU CAN'T JUST FALL A—
HER DARK CIRCLES LOOK REALLY BAD...

NEATLY TRIMMED NAILS.
WELL-GROOMED HAIR WITHOUT A SINGLE DAMAGED STRAND.
A UNIFORM WITHOUT A SPECK OF DIRT.
BY ALL APPEARANCES, SHE'S A PERFECT PRINCE...
...WHICH MAKES HER DARK CIRCLES... LIKE A SPOT ON CLEAN SHEETS...
...STICK OUT WHETHER YOU LIKE IT OR NOT.

TO GO TO THESE LENGTHS...SHE MUST WANT TO RUN AWAY FROM IT ALL, DEEP DOWN...

...BUT SHE STILL TOOK PART IN THEIR TEA PARTY WITHOUT SHOWING A SINGLE SIGN...

TELL ME...
...SAEKI-SAN. ARE YOU ALSO......?

Feelings that can't be put into words. Lips that couldn't help but touch.

No one can know these sweet, small secrets.

However......

To be continued in Volume 2...

Art Assistance

Ryousuke Kaneko
Hako Suganuma

Uniform Design Assistance

Shouko Shiga
Junko Shiga
Utako Nakamura

TRANSLATION NOTES

COMMON HONORIFICS

no honorific: Indicates familiarity or closeness; if used without permission or reason, addressing someone in this manner would constitute an insult.

-*san*: The Japanese equivalent of Mr./Mrs./Miss. If a situation calls for politeness, this is the fail-safe honorific.

-*sama*: Conveys great respect; may also indicate that the social status of the speaker is lower than that of the addressee.

-*onee-sama*: An extremely respectful way of referring to one's older sister or an older woman.

-*senpai*: A suffix used to address upperclassmen or more experienced co-workers.

PAGE 10

The class helper, or *nicchoku*, is in charge of tasks that can range from cleaning, distributing food to students during lunch, and taking attendance to assisting the teacher with the day's activities.

PAGE 16

The Japanese phrase for "deepest love" Yokozawa uses is *hyakunen no koi*, or "a love that lasts a hundred years."

Cocoon Entwined 1

Yuriko Hara

Translation: Amanda Haley • Lettering: Erin Hickman

Yen Press
150 West 30th Street, 19th Floor
New York, NY 10001

Visit us at yenpress.com • facebook.com/yenpress • twitter.com/yenpress • yenpress.tumblr.com • yenpress.com/instagram

First Yen Press Edition: July 2019

Library of Congress Control Number: 2019938438

ISBNs: 978-1-9753-8424-1 (paperback)
978-1-9753-8425-8 (ebook)

10 9 8 7 6 5 4 3 2 1

WOR

Printed in the United States of America

Yuriko Hara
1
Cocoon Entwined